T0065243

ASOUNDING MUSIC

ASOUNDING MUSIC

GERALD MIDDENTS

ASOUNDING MUSIC

iUniverse books may be ordered through booksellers or by contacting:

iUniverse
1663 Liberty Drive
Bloomington, IN 47403
www.iuniverse.com
844-349-9409

ISBN: 978-1-6632-2705-8 (sc)
ISBN: 978-1-6632-2706-5 (e)

Print information available on the last page.

iUniverse rev. date: 08/12/2021

CONTENTS

PRELUDE

Rather than composing a preface

This book will have a prelude!

This is appropriate for music

With chords doing magic!

Music and poetry are combined!

This combination now can proceed.

This book can be read in excerpts;

For both amateurs and for experts.

This book has been fun to compose;

Poetry is fitting rather than prose.

Your eyes will read these pages

Your ears may hear the notes!

Reading is for your pleasure;

You decide what to treasure!

Enjoyment will be the measure;

As you proceed at your leisure!

I. INTRODUCTION

A. MUSIC, LYRICS, MAGIC AND YOU!

What is your favorite music?

Popular? Jazz? Modern? Classic?

Does it appeal to your inner core?

Do you enjoy to hear and want more?

This poetry book will try to engage you;

Verses attempt to discover your view.

The Index identifies the range of topics,

This introduction hopefully broadens music.

Yes, winsome music is heard world-wide!

Musical notes surround us on every side!

Let us expand global music appreciation;

Melodies are universal communication!

People resonate to appealing music;

Musical vibrations have become historic!

We are brought together with our singing;

This world-wide appeal continues ringing!

The Globe includes a vast number of cultures;

Each society does have its very own practices;

Global music does have unique distinctions.

This music merits our own considerations.

HEARING IS A BRAIN FUNCTION

Our human brains process wide ranges of auditory sounds,

We have human limits surpassed by both fish and animals!

Within our heads are a pair of cochlear so very delicately,

These provide us with the sense of hearing very delightfully!

Two ears, provide capacities to locate sounds directionally,

We have capacities to detect the source almost automatically!

Permits organisms with two ears to sense reverberation locally,

Horses and dogs cock their heard to locate sounds very precisely!

These dual cochlear are crucial for sensing our environment,

Not only to hear our human species plus also many more!

Each species produces unique sounds for danger and mating!

The beautiful "Sound of Music" we humans find appealing!

Music is inspirational as vibrations stimulate our brains,

Magical perceptions known throughout all human history!

Music has profound influences upon neurons for harmony,

Likewise other species communicate with vibes intimately.

Music connects us with as a common language humanly,

    Music can speak to wide ranges of people almost universally.

Are you acquainted with anyone not having affinity for music?

    Even those who are deaf may sense these sensations pleasurably!

The universal appeal of songs in almost all human languages,

    Can have unequalled influence upon the overall human race!

This phenomenon is understood by most people inter-culturally,

    Even without understanding unique words of humans verbally.

Scientists study the unique musical calls of diverse species,

    Members in a special species discriminate their waves musically!

Sound waves intersect with our sense capacities artistically,

    Renewing our human quest for vitality and uplifting spirituality!

While we in the Western World appreciate "Amazing Grace,"

    We hope that all cultures have equivalent voice of every race.

While violent strife may be occurring in different localities,

    There are many surprises how peace is stimulated musically.

Music has the sound waves we are given from Heaven!

    We may value these beautiful waves we are given!

Now we enjoy melodies and symphonies that we hear;

    Music lifts us upward so that we value the atmosphere.

Music bridges humanity to engage in intimate communications,
This magical quality surpasses differences and disconnections.
The musical score mutually bonds diverse people with emotions,
From patriotic music nationally to romantic marriage unions!

Music has miraculous qualities to soothe conflict and hostilities,
The Russians possess inherent sensitivities to music symphonies!
Dominating Soviets intended to suppress Estonian's ambition,
But these citizens united in songfests melting the Soviet Union.

Hundreds of thousands of Estonians faced down the Soviet tanks,
Communist soldiers were emotionally gripped to become reluctant!
These nonviolent demonstrations were ended quite peacefully,
Global news reports conveyed astonishment to the world globally.

"The Sound of Music" inspired the Von Trapp family to escape,
This winsome musical drama echoed in the Austrian Landscape!
Music has inherent qualities to inspire frightened humanity,
Providing courage to face what could otherwise be a catastrophe.

We have sufficient evidence that music harmonizes universally,
Both musically within persons plus among people internationally!
To design experiments to reduce tensions among opponents personally,
Prisons have untapped potential to humanize criminals non-violently!

Religious groups have mastered how to incorporate worship music,

   Physical sports have been aroused by pep songs with unique lyrics!

Untapped possibilities await imaginations to make creative designs,

   Incorporating melodies that are harmonizing awaits new experiments!

Take note of how magically music draws crowds of people together!

   Finding the beat and rhythm plus the lyrics crowd even more cheerier!

Let your own creativity carry your musical imagination to engage,

   How people with conflicting tensions find how music can persuade!

Even initially foreign sounds may seem strange from other cultures,

   We are challenged to discover to bring people together into venues.

With a stage for original musicians to inspire people who are diverse,

   Lyric creators will blend words and sounds into harmonistic verse!

With the world-wide communications technology, what are limits?

   Is it our own creativity to discover unifying music that stimulates?

This is challenge for this age that has awareness of violent dangers,

   To avert violent conflicts with harmonizing music and magical lyrics!

B. SPECIAL MUSIC

Scripture states "The Angels Sang!" [1]

Accompanied by bells that rang!"

---

[1] The Presbyterian Hymnal, 1990, "Christmas Music," Westminster John Know Press.

Yes, Christmas Music is Angelic;

The Heavenly Hosts sang Music!

"We Three Kings from Orient Came!"

Without music, it is not the same.

Children love to do their singing,

We all love to have bells ringing!

Shepherds came to see Christ the King!

Wise Mean came from East traveling.

They all came to do their adoring;

We are inspired to go caroling!

"Consider titles of Christmas Music:

"O Little Town of Bethlehem!"

"Hark! The Heralded Angels Sing!"

Adorn Him! Adore The King!"

MOZART AND MARTIN LUTHER KING, JR.

My own mind is trying to blend

Amadeus Mozart and M.L. King, Jr.

You may wonder how this came about?

The following creation will figure this out!

While contemplating King's _Strength of Love_
I am listening to Mozart's piano concerto!
"The Piano Concerto #27 in B-flat major!"
Synthesizing phenomenal geniuses of two!

A gift was given to me upon Ordination!
King's book reported his prophetic mission!
I was fascinated in 1960 to give him regard
Unaware of that decade's turning outward!

Yes, the 1960's were a phenomenal time!
Unfolding creative activities including mine!
Exciting adventures unfurled in our society
Challenging the establishment of yesterday!

Young people caught up into new activities!
The social order loosening up with proclivities!
Generational tensions were creatively productive
Channeling them to become more constructive!

WW II and Korean War were behind us all!
Cultures opened up so as you may recall!
Youth and adults found creative tensions!
Uplifting new visions with less apprehension!

John F. Kennedy was elected our President!

He inspired the United States to be excellent!

By exploring the moon is just one illustration.

This responded to USSR space exploration!

The Cold War was a time of great tension;

EAST<>WEST were a trial for comprehension.

He had studied Mahatma Gandhi's strategies

Prompting powerful establishment processes!

Jim Lawson coached youth for demonstrations!

This magnanimous man bravely handled tensions!

Americans for freedom joined these functions!

By provoking established power into reactions!

Many people are unaware, NONVIOENCE WORKS!

In over 60 global conflicts, it has been effective!

Jesus, Gandhi and King have been proponents!

Inspiring others to become excellent exponents!

THE IMPACT OF MUSIC

How did music develop historically?

Whoever created music initially?

Did birds influence human beings?

Doing solos plus brass and strings?

How does music stimulate our brain?
Tunes do influence frame by frame!
Melodies resound in us repeatedly!
Cultures evolve music that finds fame!

Beats of drums catch our attention!
Arousing our bodies with progression!
People dance to express their rhythm!
Blending senses in our human system!

Primitive instruments along with voices,
Varieties provide people with choices!
Like birds exchange their own messages!
Repeating favorite tunes make passages!

Cultures have different instruments and tunes,
Strings, brass horns, percussion and flutes!
These unique variations sometime blend!
Vocal music has messages we may send!

Combining duets, orchestras and bands!
Voices may be solos, quartettes, trios, choirs!
Ensembles play to large audiences and march!
Societies have spontaneous preferences rehearsed!

Music is passed on from generation to the next!

We take delight by reaching what we respect!

Without music our lives would be different,

So let us eagerly encourage these benefits!

Music has been humanly conceived;

Harmonic sounds pleasantly heard!

Our ears resonate to tones of harmony;

Evoking affirmations so delightfully!

Music is usually very inspirational;

It cultivates people to be spiritual.

These emotions balance the rational,

Thereby hearers become more peaceful.

Infant children respond to sounds,

These waves resonate as pleasant.

Children may soon hum new tunes,

And enhanced by ethereal moods.

Conscious awareness is advanced,

Personal health is a resultant.

Unconscious activity contributes,

To human personality development.

Our unconscious is very complex;

Music cooks when we are at rest!

Our bodies do respond to melodies!

Listening to tunes for complexities!

THE POWER OF ENERGIZING MUSIC!

Music helps us to feel majestic!

Listeners receive a sense of magic!

Their own sensations are fantastic;

These measures are very energetic!

Dancers follow rhythms in their moves!

Their steps heighten their moods;

Audiences find music contagious.

The beats of music are delicious.

Connecting is a crucial process!

To be conceived, parents connect!

We grew in our Mother's womb

She carried us for 8-9 months!

Being born is an amazing process;

This is crucial for living creatures!

Birth involves a time of separation;

Our Mothers handled this gestation!

Mother's care is a critical factor;

As an infant in need of a helper!

As a baby, we are dependent;

We are helpless as an infant.

Each moment is important!

As infants, we need attention.

Mothers are very significant!

Because we are very dependent!

We need to be fed every day;

Our protection is their way.

Both physically and socially;

A key facet of connectivity.

Being connected is a creative factor!

Bringing people as the connector!

Persons love to join together!

Globally to become a uniter!

"Connnectivity" expands with percolation;[2]

This is also a branch of mathematics

This provides further connections

Expanding human communications.

---

[2] Houston-Edwards, K., April 2021, <u>Scientific American.</u>

Our human brains process wide ranges of auditory sounds,
We have human limits surpassed by both fish and animals!
Within our heads are a pair of cochlear so very delicately,
Providing us with a sense of hearing delightfully!

Two ears provide capacities to locate sounds directionally,
We have capacities to detect the source almost automatically!
Permits organisms with two ears to sense reverberations locally.
Horses and dogs cock their heads to locate sounds very precisely!

These dual cochlear are crucial for sensing our environment,
Not only to hear our human species plus also many more!
Each species produces unique sounds for danger and mating!
The very beautiful "Sound of Music" we find appealing!

Music is inspirational as vibrations stimulate our brains,
Magical perceptions known throughout all human history!
Music has profound influences upon neurons for harmony,
Likewise other species communicate with vibes intimately.

Music connects us with the common language humanly,
Music can speak to wife ranges of people universally.
Are you acquainted without an affinity for music?
The deaf may sense these sensations pleasurably.

The universal appeal of songs in almost all human languages,
Can have unequalled influence upon the overall human race!
This phenomena is understood by people inter-culturally.
Without understanding worlds of humans verbally.

Scientists study musical calls of diverse species,
Members of species discriminate their waves!
Sound waves intersect with our sense capacities artistically,
Renewing our human quest for vitality and uplifting spiritually.

While we in the Western World appreciate "Amazing Grace,"
We hope all cultures have equivalent voice of every race.
While violent strife may be occurring in different localities,
Surprises occur as peace is stimulated musically.

Music bridges to engage in close communications.
Magical qualities surpass differences and disconnections.
The musical score mutually bonds diverse people emotionally,
From patriotic music nationally to romantic marriage unions!

Music has miraculous qualities to soothe conflict and hostilities,
Russians possess inherent sensitivities to music symphonies!
The Soviets intended to suppress Estonian's ambition,
Citizens united in songfest melting the Soviet Union.

Then thousands of Estonians faced down tanks.

Communist soldiers were emotionally gripped reluctant!

Nonviolent demonstrations were ended quite peacefully,

Global news conveyed astonishments to the world globally.

"The Sound of Music" inspired the Von Trapp family to escape,

Winsome musical drama echoed in the Austrian landscape!

Music's inherent qualities inspire frightened humanity,

For courage to face what otherwise is catastrophe.

We have evidence music harmonizes universally,

Musically in persons plus in others internationally.

Experiments reduce tensions in opponents personally,

Prisons untap potential to humanize criminals non-violently.

Religious groups master how to incorporate worship music,

And Sports have been aroused by pep songs with lyrics.

Now possibilities await imaginations to make designs,

With melodies that harmonize new experiments.

Note how magically music draws crowds together!

With beat and rhythm plus lyrics even cheerier!

Our creativity carries our imagination to engage,

As people with conflicts find how music can persuade.

Even foreign sounds may seem strange from cultures,

We discover how to bring them together in venues.

A stage for musicians can inspires those diverse

Lyrics will blend words into harmonic verse!

World-wide communications have few limits,

Our creativity discover unifying music stimulates!

Challenging now to have awareness for dangers,

To avert conflicts with harmony and magical lyrics!

TEAMING:

When players score, they are "connecting!"

This top scoring leads to teams winning!

This requires top skills to do scoring;

Plus, competency in good coaching!

Good players attract new fans;

Crafty teams can get out of jams!

Teamwork is an enviable skill;

Together, players can "fill the bill!"

"March Madness" involves tournaments;

The best teams respond to encouragement.

This results in both winners and losers;

Plus, entertainment for supporters!

Our human brains process wide ranges of auditory sounds,

We have human limits surpassed by both fish and animals.

Within our heads are a pair of cochlear so very delicately,

Providing us with the sense of hearing delightfully!

Human beings are not the only ones who sing;

Birds of many varieties add to all those who ring.

Gibbons are also known to be singing animals;

This prompts exploration of singing mammals.

Whales are known to sing in the vast oceans;

They do make deep sound for commotions.

Insects create additional singing sounds;

They call to members of their species!

Two ears provide capacities to locate sounds directionally,

We have capacities to detect the source almost automatically!

Organisms with two ears to sense reverberation locally,

Horses cock their head to locate sounds very precisely!

These dual cochlear are crucial for sensing our environment,

Not only to hear our human species plus also many more!

All species produce unique sounds for danger and mating!

Channeling them to become constructive!

Music is inspirational as vibrations stimulate our brains,

Magical perceptions known throughout all human history!

Music has profound influences upon neurons for harmony,

Other species communicate with vibes intimately.

THE ART OF LISTENING

Listening highlights our lives;

From infant cooing to baby cries.

Our early dreams capture sounds,

Including happiness and sad frowns!

Early months we start out listening,

As our Mother might be singing!

Her voice caught our attention

She comforted our apprehension.

Yes, voices singing are comforting;

All ages levels benefit from listening.

Our brains then engage in interpreting;

As we sharpen up our own hearing.

Languages are learned by listening,

Melodies are captured with singing!

Active listening helps relationships;

Increasing our range of friendships!

The "Art of Listening" is very beneficial; [3]

In our families and careers so crucial.

Music is appreciated when listening;

Other persons value our relating!

---

[3] Nichols, M. and Straus, M., 2021, The Lost Art of Listening Guilford Press.

PEACE RESTORES PIECES

"Shalom" Jewish[4]

"Mir" Russian

"Binh" Vietnamese

"Irene" Greek

"Peace" English

"Shanti" Hindu

"Ho, Ping, An" Chinese

"Wars"

"Fights"

"Suits"

"Battles"

"Disputes"

"Conflicts"

"Disagreement"

"Table"

"Treaty"

"Smile"

"Candle"

"Settlement"

"Handshake"

"Settlement"

"Assaults"

"Invasions"

"Divorce"

"Struggles"

"Controversies"

"Lawlessness"

"Family Fights"

---

[4] Psalm 29: 11; 34: 14, Isaiah 26: 3; John 14: 27; I Corinthians 7: 15; Ephesians 2: 14; I Peter 3: 11: I Timothy 2: 2.

II. MY PERSONAL CONNECTIONS

My roots go back to my birth in 1933

Of course, this is not in my memory.

My family appreciated musicality;

They introduced me very readily.

Yes, we had an upright piano;

My Mother could play in solo.

My Father loved to sing baritone!

Earlier he also played the violin.

My older brother played the trumpet!

He played it in bands for high school.

My older sister played the piano;

So, she was my first instructor!

During fifth grade piano lessons;

Mrs. Tubbs was my instructor.

She was professionally educated;

Lessons required me to practice.

Playing the piano was very valuable;

My own coordination was required.

After early years, came the classics;

Themes of Bach and Beethoven.

The piano is an amazing instrument!

For solos and also as accompaniment.

Hearers do express their appreciation,

Whether modern score or from tradition.

The piano is also very versatile,

Key for a wide range of sounds!

Few instruments have these vibrations!

Players and hearers find sensations!

I also learned popular music;

Plus, hymns sung in our churches.

Singing in Choirs also developed:

In Schools, Colleges and Liturgies.

The piano is an amazing instrument!

For solos and also as accompiament!

Hearers do express their appreciation

Whether modern score or from tradition.

The piano is also very versatile

Keys for a wide range of sounds!

The keyboard is readily learned

Compositions valued if composed.

Compositions created as celebrations;

Or loss of loved one for as recollections.

Scores designed for our contemplation;

The composers merit our recognition.

Modern keyboards are now widely played;

Electrical precisions are being recognized!

Grand pianos are now often preferred

Large in dimensions but very revered!

MUSIC AND MEDIA

Music is a medium to set moods;

It serves us as the artistic foods!

We have preferences for flavors;

We miss music if sounds waver!

Excitement with fast tempos;

Somber music for our sadness.

Accented pace goes rapidly!

Sports' beats go excitedly!

Movies have fitting background;

Our moods connect to sounds.

Music affects our heartbeats;

Emotions provide full treats!

Dramas are also very engaging;

We are caught up when watching!

Melodies stick for our repeating;

Lyrics help us do remembering!

Carol and I have special recollections!

Our wedding Prelude by Mary Preston!

Organ for "Jesu, Joy of Man's Desiring!"[5]

Victor Hansen was also accompanying!

This leads into our wedding procession;

Guests experienced a warm welcoming!

This was our exciting occasion for matching!

In our memory, this music is everlasting!

A. MUSIC FOR BETTER HEALTH

Here is an excellent contemporary illustration;

It is about a virus patient in hospitalization.

The television photos showed near his bed;

Playing his violin for the hospital staff.[6]

This patient has tubes in his throat;

Prohibiting him from opening his mouth

---

[5] Bach, Johann Sebastian was the famous compower.
[6] Public Television news on November 19, 2020.

He has a smile on his face while playing;

The Nurses and Doctors are listening!

What a wonderful way to communicate!

Music provides melodies to appreciate!

His violin music provided an alternative;

Instrumental music expresses good motives.

We humans learn new ways to be expressive;

Eyes and ears help us become restorative.

Talented musicians are also imaginative

Helping humanity to be appreciative!

MUSIC THERAPY

Music possesses capacities for healing; [7]

Another reason to find it appealing.

Our ears resonate to this quality

Helping our brains to live healthy!

Music therapy is medically helpful;

Especially melodies we find special!

Esperanza Spalding is a new pioneer

She created music called "12 Little Spells."

---

[7] Moore, M., April 2, 2021, "Her Quest is for Musical Healing, The New York Times.

Each "Spell" helps different body parts!

Spalding discovers these healing arts.

Humanity has cultivated this therapy

We can also refine it more helpfully.

Musical waves stimulate the cochlear

This is where sounds strike the ear.

One's brain interprets different tones

Combinations together make the tunes.

Two ears help detect sound location

Conductors are aware of sensations.

This also facilitates their conducting

As they balance who is contributing.

BEYONDER-MENTS

Let me de-mystify BEYONDER-MENTS!

This idea is related to WONDER-MENTS!

It is derived from the adverb "BEYOND!"

Which is also connected to "WONDER!"

Poetically, we "wonder" and also reflect!

Prayerfully, we wonder about" beyonder!"

Beyonder infers visions which we wonder!

Beyonders are persons who go further!

Further than we ordinarily imagine!

We might connect these to "Evangel!"

This takes us to the realm of good news!

Trying to comprehend more of God's views!

God stretches us to envision "beyondering!"

To suggests mysteries beyond wondering!

God promises that we will have eternal life!

Which is beyond the limits of earthly strife!

For a "BEYONDERING-MOMENT" here & now!

Prayerfully close your eyes and let your head bow!

Focus upon what heaven may mean to you!

"Beyonder-Moments" will help us renew!

Beyond here and now to there and then!

Permit your imagination to then venture!

Now let you mind invite heavenly images

That beckon you to have faithful visions!

Take time so "The Mind of Christ" unfolds!

As you ponder favorite Biblical promises!

You may be invited to "BEYONDER-MENTS!"

That profoundly deepen your faithfulness!

Ponder and Wonder what heaven is like

Drawing you Beyond what is after this life!

"WONDERMENTS!"

We live in God's amazing universe that we attempt to behold!

  His awesome Wonderments continue to continuously unfold!

With our awareness that this very universe is God's creation,

  We are privileged to be living in His Presence of origination!

How might we respond to acknowledge this very recognition?

  That we are His Creatures who are existing in His Creation?

Yes, we are infinitesimal in Our God's own imaginative world

  This simple awareness recognizes how living creatures unfurl!

We are awed with the expanse of time and space that now exists!

  Rejoicing that we now are privileged to be alive and also persist!

O God, You provide us with conscious awareness to acknowledge

  You are our God and moreover, we are your special people!

In our Wonderments, we realize that we have our responsibilities,

  As we are trusted stewards to be respectful of more possibilities!

Let us refresh our pledge to honorably preserve this universe!

  Realizing future generations depend upon how we preserve!

May we conserve this earth and billions of other human beings,

  To jointly enhance this environment for generations to be living!

This undertaking is an over-whelming expectation for creatures,

  But we pledge by committing ourselves for new world futures!

As cosmology explores the further boundaries of this universe,
　　　　New data are challenging previous theories of Time and Space.
Closed systems are not adequate to explain new discoveries,
　　　　Scientists are constantly amazed to develop new theories!

Terms that come to mind from human language seem limited,
　　　　These expansive findings invite new terms to be invented.
"Awesome" and "Amazements" suggest concepts to enlarge,
　　　　Now "WONDERMENTS" enter our own vocabulary as novel!

"WONDERMENTS" suggest these astonishing new findings,
　　　　Inviting original thinking that tells about fresh happenings.
Imaginative reflections prompt ideas about our environment,
　　　　How was this "Multi-verse" created as infinite development?

Literature designed to account for the Originator of creation,
　　　　Includes Genesis One this came "out of nothing" "ex-nihilo!"
God created Light for us to see and Darkness when we sleep,
　　　　This daily rhythm is essential for the growth of creatures.

All forms of human explorations involve an intelligent brain,
　　　　This key organ requires rest to rejuvenate to counter strain.
Life on Earth functions best in cycles of activity and also rest,
　　　　Rather than taking this for granted, we see we are blessed.

Reflective thinking increases our awareness of this creation,
　　　"WONDERMENTS" partially captures our new fascination.
The extent of this multi-verse may be beyond our capacities,
　　　Prompting creative processes tickling our new curiosities.

Restlessness ignites both new investigations and knowledge,
　　　Searching for accurate descriptions approximating truth.
These discoveries will contribute to our human appreciations,
　　　Expanding our wisdom about our unique place in creation!

Now Scientists propose "The Big Bang" as a hypothesis,
　　　Erupting about 13.6 billion years ago as the beginning!
Now the multi-verses have since been thereby created,
　　　While continuing to expand as a "BEYONDERMENT!"

These are very exciting recent scientific explanations,
　　　Inviting more continuous research about creations,
The awareness of these possibilities is very exciting
　　　So that more human awareness is also igniting!

Are there also now creatures with intelligent faculties?
　　　And will such plausible creatures also be engaging?
We hopefully will pursue Theology and also Cosmology,
　　　While we all cultivate additional human curiosities!

With your assurance of helping us to be humanly responsible

We reply upon You who entrusts us for creation to be viable!

When we feel inadequate, O Lord, please provide us assistance

So that Earth and Your Universe have dependable persistence.

B. CROSS CULTURAL MUSIC

Bridging cultures readily occurs with music;

Musical tones and words have magic!

Music resonates in our human ears

To comfort, support and cheers!

Yo Yo Ma plays his own special cello; [8]

Responsiveness from gals and fellows!

YoY o Ma takes his Bach concerts

To all of Earth's six continents!

He also generates wide awareness

Of diverse environmental concerns!

He promotes social justice issues

As he has concerns about planets!

Yo Yo also tries to assuage discord,

To strengthen community bonds.

---

[8] Kale, Claudia, May 2021, "Bridging Cultures and Good Causes with Music," National Geographic.

This demonstrates musical appeals;

So that humanity learns how to yield!

The Chinese culture values their music;

While in Beijing, I attending an opera.

While their language is foreign to me;

I wanted both to hear and to see.

Their opera production was appreciated;

The cast was non-verbal as it communicated.

The music in China is also State-Approved [9]

Now celebrating the State 100th Anniversary.

Chinese Communism is intentionally patriotic;

They honor the long march of 1000 miles.

In 2021, 300 operas, ballets and musicals

Engage the Chinese to be participants.

Cultures readily create their own music;

Expressing tones and also new lyrics.

People can sing and play instruments;

They can also dance special movements.

[9] Hernanadez, J., July 2, 2021, :State-Approved Music Fills Lineup of Events,"
New York Times.

Lyrics often express our deep emotions;

Both secular and religious devotions.

With the words that constitute hymns!

Plus, cultural and national anthems!

Many holidays have special music;

Christmas is particularly expressive.
Children really enjoy this special day;
Hoping Santa Claus comes their way.

"O PERFECT LOVE"

Hymns have become very influential;

They stimulate my poetry potential!

Hymns are very powerful to sing;

Uplifting, hymns do have wings![10]

"Jesus Loves Me!" This I Know!"

As a child, I sang this as a solo!

Now as Minister for 800+ times,

I notice how the verses rhyme!

When planning worship services,

First hymn selected is "Adoration!"

The middle hymn for contemplation;

Closing hymn strengthens motivation!

---

[10] Psalm 23; Romans 8: 31-39; John 14: 1-14.

Yes, these are among my favorites!

I recommend hymns to contemplate!

"O Love That Wilt Not Let Me Go" [11]

Affirming my Faith, I Love to Know!

LOVING KINDNESS

Mothers we know demonstrate to us their loving kindness!

They are the key relation for us to learn trustworthiness!

Jointly with Fathers we experience dedicated faithfulness!

Together, they may correct us with their steadfast justice!

In God's Very Presence we come to appreciate his holiness!

As we grow in our faith in God, we experience forgiveness!

Maturing in faith we also appreciate Jesus' graciousness

Jointly, we are uplifted by his humbleness and helpfulness!

Together in the Church Community, we show relatedness!

Supporting each other, we express God's loving kindness!

As we go forth into the world, we depend upon His justice!

Reaching out to the ill and the bereaved into their loneliness!

Empowered by the Holy Spirit to extend! our inclusiveness!

Addressing errors in society for expressing exclusiveness!

We are renewed in our mission to show Jesus' friendliness!

To those who are experiencing hardships and also sickness!

---

[11] Psalm 107 gives attention to "Unfailing Love" six times.

Our parents, especially, our Mother taught us loving kindness!

Treasured deeply inside us, we find our special assuredness!

Inspired to engage in working and sharing God's Faithfulness!

Our hearts are restless until we find in Him our eternal rest![12]

MOZART AND MARTIN LUTHER KING, JR

My mind is trying to blend

Amadeus Mozart and ML King, Jr.

You may wonder how this came about?

The following creation will figure this out!

While contemplating King's Strength of Love

I am listening to Mozart's piano concerto!

"The Piano Concerto #27 in B-flat major!

Synthesizing phenomenal geniuses of two!

A gift was given to me upon Ordination!

King's book reported his prophetic mission!

I was fascinated in 1960 to give him regard

Unaware of that decade's turning outward!

Yes, the 1960's were a phenomenal time!

Unfolding creative activities including mine!

Exciting adventures unfurled in our society

Challenging the establishment of yesterday!

---

[12] Confessions of St. Augustine. Plus Ruth 2: 14-23 and Titus 3: 4-6.

Young people caught up into new activities!

The social order loosening up with proclivities!

Generational tensions were creatively productive

Channeling them to become constructive!

WW II and Korean War were behind us all!

Cultures opened up so as you may recall!

Youth and adults found creative tensions!

Uplifting new visions with less apprehension!

John F. Kennedy was elected our President!

He inspired the United States to be excellent!

By exploring the moon is just one illustration

This responded to USSR space exploration!

His assassination became a global tragedy!

While focusing efforts as a power globally!

Tensions of the Cold War were frightening

American creativity was quickly unfolding!

During my initial ministry in Minnetonka!

Inspiration came further to be a Professor!

Inter-disciplinary studies I than did prefer

Theology<>Psychology two field that were!

MOZART: THE REIGN OF LOVE!

At age six, he was already a prodigy!

His instrument was the clavier!

He also played in Austrian Church.

He accompanied Mass readily

In 1763, Officials were astonished!

Mozart played the organ for worship!

At eight, he composed a symphony!

"Every day God performs fresh miracles!

Mozart's precocity as a youth was noticed;

Classical music was his key expression!

He claimed this was also effortless;

Compositions almost write themselves!

His drafts often needed no revisions!

He also played for the opera stage!

He was fundamentally a happy man!

He also enjoyed a loving marriage!

"The Marriage of Figaro" composed;

"Quicksilver brightness" energetically!

Mozart was almost indefatigable!

He possessed divine comedy![13]

---

[13] Swafford, J., "Mozart: The Reign of Love," Faber and Fabers.

In the Middles Ages, Churches had organs

Now organs dominate Church music!

In Russia, antiphonal choirs sing;

Balconies sing back and forth!

C. RELATING SCIENCE AND RELIGION

My denomination had funds and vision!

Providing fellowships blending with religion!

My synthesis "To understand God theologically

With my understanding of people psychologically!"

Fortunately, I my mentor, E. Paul Torrance

Internationally known for creativity research!

Serving as his research and teaching assistant

Enriched comprehension of creative processes!

In 1965, I heard Dr. Martin Luther King speak!

His inspirational messages were very prophetic!

Risking his life in demonstrations and prisons

He made unforgettable personal impressions!

King had integrated his ideas of nonviolence!

Leading peaceful marches without arrogance!

He had studied Mahatma Gandhi's strategies

Prompting powerful establishment processes!

Jim Lawson coached youth for demonstrations!

This magnanimous man bravely handled tensions!

Americans for freedom joined these functions!

By provoking established power into reactions

MUSIC WHILE DREAMING

We may not recall these dreams awaking,

As they usually occur in early sleeping.

Our most recent dreams before waking,

Quickly vanishing without quick recording.

Poets anguish about their ecstatic visions,

Unaware of their cognitions and emotions.

Upon valuing these revelations in sleep,

They enrich poetry by fathoming the deep.

Deep breathing often accompanies dreams,

Poetry is always been about our breathing!

Latin terms help to understand "inspire!"

"In" plus "spirare" produces inspirations!

"Poetry is a way of taking life by the throat!"

These are Robert Frost's own descriptions.

Spear states "meaning from sleeplessness."

"Acquainted with the night: Insomnia Poems!"

RECENT INVESTIGATIONS

Neuroscience recognizes value of sleep,
>   While creative persons discover the deep!
Our brains need rest but are half awake,
>   Our bodies are still, but minds are inspired.

My personal accounts value my dreaming,
>   While I am puzzled by prizes revealing!
The human brain is a universe to explore,
>   With contours, peaks and valleys for sure.

Waking in wee hours half consciousness,
>   Insights can be mined for wakefulness!
We may discover value in sleeplessness.
>   Unfolding insights known as wistfulness!

Researchers extend artificial intelligence;
>   To create music now with their evidence!
They are trying to produce new formulas,
>   To write new music for full orchestras!

They are discovering patterns of sounds,
>   That extend from these new formulas.
Difficulties are encountered immediately
>   To make equations the music accurately.

Creative musicians have nuances in music

That formula cannot write mechanically.

This challenges current artificial intelligence

As creativity out-maneuvers very readily!

Statistical equations encounter limits;

Much like: "Play it again, Nikita!"[14]

Creative dimensions are neglected;

Await challenges to be invented.

NONVIOLENT EFFECTIVENESS

Yes, John, I may have Wilson/Lightman hid in dark cellars,

But right now I am in Sherman without access into my silos!

So to keep me off the streets then I walk in Fairview Park,

I had a consultation with sources older than all of us kids!

The attachment grew to eight pages long with no sweat,

You better go to the bathroom before you undertake it!

At our wedding at King of Glory Church back in 1993,

My parsons from Sherman gave advice to "congregations!"

"You people don't know Jerry very well, I can appreciate,

You can get into conversations with him to go endlessly!

---

[14] "Composing by Computer; Programmes by Programs," <u>The Economist</u>, June 5, 2021.

"*Be sure that you go to the bathroom first!*" he advised,

    So, I am sharing this advice before you get more involved!

Patrick went to Oklahoma State in the 1970's way back,

    His last name is McCoy, he was studying to be a journalist,

If you had him in class, Bob, he has an inviting smile,

    One that is memorable plus his clever twists and turns.

Patrickand Henry are colleagues from Princeton Seminary,

    They had my late wife's memorial service in, May, 1988!

Henry also has a Ph.D. from Wisconsin U. about Africa,

    Patrick ministered at a growing church in McKinney.

Now watch out when you get entangled with psychologists,

    Maybe a Freudian, Jungian, Behavioralist or Existentialist!

We do not know much about outer space or endless time,

    Because, we are suppose to dig into the space of our brains!

Jung suggested a 100 years ago breaking off with Freud,

    The universe "out there" has another parallel here on earth!

This is the trillion neurons bouncing in our body around,

    Controlled by our brains that has space still unexplored!

So, neurosciences are endeavoring to comprehend,

    But so much is still unknown in our complex systems.

Let's keep on racking our neurons bouncing around,
    Maybe we need to get bigger caps to hold heads on!

OK, a few minutes ago I fertilized our flowers in front,
    Now I better water them or continue to do rain dances!
I know you people do not really believe these claims,
    Any doubts you have will preclude that your get rains!

I only charge by cookies to perform this special magic,
    So, you better get to your kitchen oven plus mixing it up.
From the dryer states in the country, calls every day,
    If you want to learn the five steps, better sign up today!

These procedures are founded by Native Americans,
    Who used only the natural resources for their programs!
These Natural Scientists combined with Socio-Biologists,
    Creating steps in harmony with many primary polygamists.

D. CHILDREN HAVE QUESTIONS!

I want to know?
    Where do you go?
      When you leave home?

Do you go to work?

Or go to the store?

Will you bring more?

Do you have fun?

What do you run?

Indoors or in the sun?

Who do you work with?

Do you work in shifts?

Will you bring me gifts?

Can I go with you?

Will I find it new?

What might I do?

What will I learn?

Is your boss stern?

Will I be a concern?

Am I old enough?

Am I also tough?

Is the future rough?

Do you get food?

So, will it be good?

Are toothpicks wood?

What about dissent?

Does eating hurt?

Will I be alert?

THE IMPACT OF MUSIC

How did music develop historically?

Whoever created music initially?

Did birds influence human beings?

Doing solos plus brass and strings?

How does music stimulate our brain?

Tunes do influence frame by frame!

Melodies resound in us repeatedly!

Cultures evolve music that finds fame!

Beats of drums catch our attention!

Arousing our bodies with progression!

People dance to express their rhythm!

Blending senses in our human system!

Primitive instruments along with voices,

Varieties provide people with choices!

Like birds exchange their own messages!

Repeating favorite tunes make passages!

Cultures have different instruments and tunes,

Strings, brass horns, percussion and flutes!

These unique variations sometime blend!

Vocal music has messages we may send!

Composed of duets, orchestras and bands!

Voices may be solos, quartettes, trios and choirs!

Ensembles play to the large audiences and march!

Societies have spontaneous preferences rehearsed!

Music is passed on from generation to the next!

We take delight by reaching what we respect!

Without music our lives would be different,

Let us eagerly encourage these benefits!

When words fail, music can speak![15]

---

[15] Levitin, D., 8/25, 2016, "Where Word Fail, Music Speaks,"

CHRISTMAS MUSIC INSPIRES

Scriptures state "The Angels Sang!" [16]

Accompanies by bells that rang!

Yes, Christmas Music is Angelic

The Heavenly Hosts sang music!

"We Three Kings from Orient Came."

Without music, it is not the same.

Children love to engage in singing;

We all love to have the bells ringing!

Shepherds came to see Christ the King!

Wise Men came from afar traveling!

They all came to do their adoring;

We are expected to go caroling!

Consider the titles of Christmas Music:

"O Little Town of Bethlehem!"

"Hark! The Heralded Angels Sing!"

"Adore Him! Adore the King!"

Major productions as "The Messiah!"

"Come, Thou Long-Expected Jesus!"

---

[16] <u>The Presbyterian Hymnal,</u> 1990, "Christmas Music, Westminster John Knox Press.

"Comfort, Comfort You, My People;"

"Jesus Comes with Clouds Descending!"

"Let All Mortal Flesh Keep Silent!"

"Silent Night! Holy Night!" repeated;

"Lift Up You Heads; Ye Mighty Gates!"

"O Come, O Come, Emmanuel!"

"Watchman, Tell Us of the Night!"

"Angels from the Realms of Glory!"

"Angels We Have Heard on High!"

"Break Forth, O Beauteous Heavenly Light!"

"Away in a Manger!" we often sing;

And "Gentle Mary Laid Her Child!"

"Good Christian Friends Rejoice!"

We know all of these, of course.

"In Bethlehem, a Babe Was Born!"

"In Bethlehem a Newborn Boy!"

"It Came Upon the Midnight Clear!"

Plus "Joyful Christmas Day is Here!"

Echoing--"Joy to the World!"

"O Come All Ys Faithful!"

"O Sleep, Dear Holy Baby!"

"On this Day Earth Shall Ring!"

"Lo, how a Rose E'er Blooming!"

"While Shepherds Watched Their Flocks!"

"T'was, in the Midst of Wintertime!"

And *"Once, in Royal David's City!*

MUSICAL SCORE: *D EFLAT-G-F-BFLAT-D-EFLAT.*

What do you know?----we have the Spacers!

This is a pleasant surprise for US Earthers!

We have questions for these Spacers:

Who is Listening?

Can You Hear Us?

We are all part of this Universe

We need the time to rehearse!

We Earthers are glad Spacers came to visit us!

Joy, beautiful spark of Divinity [or gods],

Daughter of <u>Elysium</u>,

We enter, drunk with fire,

Heavenly one, thy sanctuary!

Thy magic binds again

What custom strictly divided;*

All people become brothers,*

Where thy gentle wing abides.

Whoever has succeeded in the great attempt,

To be a friend's friend,

Whoever has won a lovely woman,

Add his to the jubilation!

Yes, and also whoever has just one soul

To call his own in this world!

And he who never managed it should slink

Weeping from this union!

All creatures drink of joy

At nature's breasts.

All the Just, all the Evil

Follow her trail of roses.

Kisses she gave us and grapevines,

A friend, proven in death.

Salaciousness was given to the worm

And the cherub stands before God.

Gladly, as His suns fly

through the heaven's ground plan

Joy, beautiful spark of Divinity [or: of gods],

Daughter of Elysium,

We enter, drunk with fire,

Heavenly one, thy sanctuary!

Thy magic binds again

What custom strictly divided; *

All people become brothers, *

Where thy gentle wing abides.

Whoever has succeeded in the great attempt,

To be a friend's friend,

Whoever has won a lovely woman,

Add his to the jubilation!

Yes, and also whoever has just one soul

To call his own in this world!

And he who never managed it should slink

Weeping from this union!

All creatures drink of joy

At nature's breasts.

All the Just, all the Evil

Follow her trail of roses.

Kisses she gave us and grapevines,

A friend, proven in death.

Salaciousness was given to the worm

And the cherub stands before God.

Gladly, as His suns fly

through the heavens' grand plan

III. WHO BEGETS PEACE?

A. NEED FOR HARMONY

Creation lodges some strange creatures!

A number possess belligerent features!

Ready to display their own tempers!

Using violence to quickly conquer!

Evolutionary explanations are stated

in a word: "The survival of the fittest!"

Is this describing how to be vicious?

Accounting why to become malicious?

"An eye for an eye?" "Tooth for Tooth?"

Revenge results in one who is uncouth!

This creature to be the last survivor?

So, this is one who remains alive?

WHAT ELSE?

Why do species continue to exist?

What are the clues to still persist?

Evolution has major limitations!

The survivors provoke explanations!

Could there be extensive reproduction?

    By multiplying faster than extinction?

Humans grow 5, to 6, to 7, to 10 billion!

    Can the earth support up to 12 billion?

Humans benefit from acting globally!

    Consumption affects others personally!

Earth's environment also needs care!

    Conserving so everyone is able to share!

MATING OF PEACE<>VIOLENCE

Does violence beget more violence?

    Civil respect is basically advocated!

Violence is predominantly masculine!

    Peace is primarily more feminine!

Violence typically dominates mates!

    Victims persist on abuse and hate!

Aggression wants to be alpha males

    Frequently beyond a fitting scale!

Abusive violence is passed forward!

    To descendants who live afterward

Peace survives horrible conditions!

    Hesitant to leave without protection!

Efforts to reconcile are so tentative!

    Safety jeopardized as being negative!

Violence needs to become managed!

    The interests of all those connected!

WHO BEGETS WHOM?

Overcoming violence and begetting violence!

    More civil respect is readily advocated!

Peace needs both strength and fortitude!

    Violence controls behavior and attitudes!

Violence breeds more violent behavior!

    People react to being threatened and hurt!

This awareness creative few alternatives!

    Peace generates from human responses!

Nonviolence requires real commitment!

    Disciplined reactions become apparent!

Pinker[17] discovered decreasing violence!

    Confirmed by Armstrong's evidence![18]

---

[17] Pinker,
[18] Armstrong, Karen

B. GLOBAL HUMANITY

Humanity also is part of environment!

 Needing to conserve takes discernment!

Protecting natural resources is essential!

 Otherwise, lives cannot reach potential!

Peace deliberately becomes protective!

 Most humanity wants to be proactive!

Peace begetting peaceful nonviolence

 Leading us forward to then advance!

Offspringing from peace is "civility!"

 This contributes to everyone globally!

Humanity needs to manage animals,

 Contributing respect to environment!

Persons can also unite musically,

 Irrespective of their nationality.

Global humanity needs peace

 To overcome violent strife.

We can pursue "connectivity!"

 As now this is needed globally.

Peace and justice are companions

 Demonstrating universal re-union.

Together if taking steps gracefully

    Adults teaching youth educationally.

As, old hostilities can be overcome;

    To discover peaceful values as one!

    The futures could unfold more unified;

        Rather than tensions that collide1

    Persons would not choose a side

        But benefit from harmony to reside!

1

UNIFYING MUSIC

    Why is music for eons cross-cultural?

        What makes music arouse us so special?

    Music tingles inside our own head-----

        Melodies feed our appetites like bread!

    Brains are inherently stimulated by music!

        Dancing in our craniums to become effective1

    Each culture has its favorite melodies,

        Enhanced by drumbeats plus harmonies!

    Hearing familiar music is pleasurable!

        We are uplifted by our musical heritage!

    Playing an instrument is also uplifting,

        These musical scores are very enhancing1

We too, can be involved when we sing

    Multiplying pleasures by our contributing!

Singing and playing plus also listening

    Prompts our own brains to be appreciating!

We are pleased with musical resonance,

    Welcoming symphonies also does enhance!

Listening and playing are human interests,

    Advancing appreciations for our instruments!

Musicians provide us with special gifts!

    Along with the addition of rhyming lyrics1

Human creativity is a wonderful talent,

    That enriches our own lives to be valiant!

Andrea Bucelli, who is a blind vocalist,

    With his wife and also as a soloist,

His own voice is a gift for humanity

    As a soloist or even as a symphony!

This Bucelli couple resonate;

    They know how to celebrate!

GLOBAL ANTHEM[19]

Citizens of <u>GAIA</u>, our Mother Earth,

We have known you since our birth!

As teammates on this Created Earth,

We give our gratitude for our worth.

As we live in this time and this space,

Teammates know this is our place.

Our words give Mother Earth honor,

To YOU our respect we now offer!

Gravity holds planets here together

As athletes, we thank our Creator.

Orientals and Occidentals on Earth!

Spanning from South also North!

Respecting opponents and teammates,

We grow mutually as true athletes.

We live in justice and in harmony,

Peaceful is just how we want to be!

We are not here on Gaia accidentally,

Believe in God's own intentionality!

---

[19] Middents, G., 2004, Sung at the Global Meeting of the Organizational Development Institute, U. of Colima, Mx.

As athletes we are willing to sacrifice,
We know that He paid for our price!

In discipline, you are our neighbors,
Loving You, we hope as You do us.
Jointly we can help Gaia peacefully,
Ethically doing justice sustainably.

Where our words fail, music speaks!
Enhanced by more proactive peace!
Hearers arrest conflicts while listening
Humans are calmed while singing!

When words are not enough, music helps!
It places life where words cannot reach!
Music introduces us to heavenly calm!
When fractured humans need a balm!

MANY ANTHEMS

Anthems are widely composed
Sung in verses by members!
These express profound loyalties;
Voice by the members vocally!

National Anthems are well known;

Members have their voices shown!

States within nations are loyal;

Earth citizens are also vocal!

Educational institutions express music;

Universities and colleges have lyrics!

High Schools sing with enthusiasm;

By supporting teams with expressions!

This music expresses their harmony;

Competitors know about this loyalty!

Hymns are also readily learned;

Words are quickly memorized!

Henry James advice to his son:

1. Be Kind!

2. Be Kind!

3. Be Kind!

Jesus' Advice to Followers:

1. Express Loving-Kindness!

2. Express Loving Kindness!

3. Express Loving-Kindness!

C. PEACE AND JUSTICE MARRY!

Remember "The Brute" so violent?
  He is also known as the Rapist!
His wife, Peace, and their offspring;
  Fear as he comes home drinking!

Peace wonders "if this is enough?"
  She hopes she and kids can be tough
Is family life going to be this rough?
  Peace wonders how we can get out?

  Police protection does not work!
    As a wife and mother not to shirk!
  Then she learns how to be rescued!
    Domestic Abuse was the Avenue!

  Peace leaves Violence as a failure!
    She finds safety for her amd children!
  Leaving him for a life of their own!
    They discover they are not alone!

NEW HOPE

A year goes on in rehabilitation!
  Learning to overcome manipulation!
"Foxy Violence" was tough to leave
  Who can be trusted not to deceive?

Wars become another dead-end!
  Peace keeps trying to find a friend!
"Who is this other guy, Justice?"
  Are his ideals to become trusted!

Justice requests: "Can we be friends?"
  Peace takes a chance for her children!
She discovers Justice, a genuine guy!
  Their romance is quickly able to fly!

Marriage of Peace and Justice occurs!
  Her kids learn "Justice is Trusted!"
They try to forget about Violence
  In time, they develop a conscience!

A year passes in rehabilitation
  Learning to overcome manipulation!
Foxy Violence was tough to leave!
  Who can be trusted and not deceived?

Wars become another "dead-end!"

    Peace keeps trying to find a friend.

"Who is this young guy, Justice?"

    Are his ideals able to be trusted?

Justice asks: "Can we be friends?"

    Peace takes a chance for her children!

She discovers Justice a genuine guy!

    Their romance is so very able to fly!

Marriage of Peace<>Justice occurs

    Her kids learn Justice is trusted!

They try to forget about Violence.

    In time, they develop a conscience!

This couple is pestered by Violence!

    He is a tough with a long persistence!

When will he eventually subside?

    Violence does not want to be denied!

Humanity continues this long struggle!

    Knowing people do not live in a bubble!

Violence has offspring in many places!

    So conflicts continue without relieving!

How long will humanity be suckered?

    Vulnerable to old Violence as offered!

Peace beyond human understanding!

    With Justice with her for protecting!

WORTHY FIRST STARTS!

The League of Nations, 20th century

    Launched ideals that were worthy!

But human limitations showed up

    It did not last as an initial start-up!

After WW II, The United Nation begins!

    Bringing together many global forces!

Its agenda is for World Peace for all

    Worthy efforts help and also fail!

"The World Court" has been launched!

    Sternly addressing the crimes of war!

But The United States has held out!

    Politically now willing to lose clout!

As stated before, violence is declining!

    But continues in attempts to be reigning!

However, Peace and Justice are providing

    Basic alternatives for Peace-Building!

Humanity needs help from outside!

Divine Justice comes to then abide!

People plea for Justice to prevail!

Hope provides in how to triumph!

Experiments that are cross-cultural

Attract global people who are diverse!

Blending ideals from other traditions

Assisting Peace and Justice transitions!

THE LION AND THE LAMB!

Here is an ideal of Western cultures!

That may appeal to global justice!

Universal concepts need balance

To provide world-wide acceptance!

They shall eventually lay together![20]

Rather than be victim and victor!

This "Kingdom of Peace" awaits

As God Almighty's future promise!

Then visions can draw us forward!

To pursue pathways going upward!

Someday, Somewhere, Somehow!

Draws humanity into tomorrow!

---

[20] Isaiah

Fear and anxiety will also be reduced!

Establishing that violence has no use!

Peace and Justice will then preside!

In atmospheres where all can thrive!

PIANO PROMINENCE

Why is the piano the premier musical instruments?

In my opinion, in musical spheres it has no equivalent!

Historically, piano was developed about 300 years ago!

It has risen quickly to prominence in home and also solo.

Mastering the piano demands immense virtuosity!

A pianist's brain processes the sounds of audiology!

Equally significant is command of manual dexterity,

The intricate coordination of ten fingers requires ingenuity!

In addition, touching this complex keyboard is essential,

Very sensitive feeling is needed to reach one's potential!

There are rare blind pianists, but they are an exception,

Very perceptive vision in order to play is an expectation!

The coordination of all senses is used in performances,
　　　Including kinesthetic mastery of tendons and also muscles!

Few persons recognize the key role of one's vestibular!
　　　This involves balance in order to be upright and vertical!

Vision, hearing, tactile and brain neurons then function,
　　　Olfactory sense for smelling likely engages in collaboration!

Pianists process intricate capacity for immense memory!
　　　Trillions of neurological transmitters occur simultaneously!

CONSIDERING COMPARABLES

Can you identify other instruments that are so versatile?
　　　Major combinations of notes can be included with a smile!

Even a symphony orchestra conductor will recognize
　　　The ultra-complexity that pianists are able to contribute!

A pianist and orchestra jointly perform amazingly,
　　　The most demanding role is upon the pianist playing!

Pianists incorporate multiple symphonic sounds,
　　　Compositions for both piano and orchestra are renown!

The pipe organ is in this category of keyboard skills,
  Both have parallel keyboards for controlling the chords!

Yes, the organist has many pipes at their command,
  The mechanics of both are complex but differentiated!

Mastery of both organ and piano is complementary,
  Specialists are reluctant to play both even temporarily!
  .

Both the sounds and tactile sensations are distinctive,
  Very find qualities contribute to making them unique!

Bach's compositions and scores are designed for organ!
  While Bach can also be performed on piano keyboards!

A unique feature of an organ is about foot pedals,
  These provide tones that have immense auditory sounds,

The piano and organ provide the melodious of chords,
  They resound the highest complexity for performances!

Composers provide considerably more piano selections,
  The widest range of sounds is available for human hearing.

Both piano and organ are also electronically constructed.
  The last century complex electronic technology developed!

The sounds of strings and pipes are distinguishable,

These electronic keyboards provide greater ease available!

Within the realm of feasibility is another technique,

Implanted transistors in human brains may be equivalent!

Humans also have a limited range of sensing sounds!

Other creatures possess lower and higher competencies.

Digital transpositions can provide visual representations,

However, the natural human range is our limit in creation!

PIANO AS EXCEPTIONAL

Over half of millennia composers have been challenged,

The refinement of piano construction has also excelled!

Modern composers are now originating new chords,

Algorithms facilitate exceptionally creative sounds!

Competition for composers and performers are elevating,

Possibilities are discovered with new dissonant recordings!

The obvious contrasts with pop music are astounding!

While piano continues to appeal to be very outstanding!

The contemporary aspirants seek recognition early,
    Inspiring and challenging them to practice thoroughly!

Emerging talent demonstrates very delicate techniques,
    Assuring that audiences will be hearing players unique!

The future promises to be exciting for us to admire!
    As young students are trained and disciplined to aspire!

D. POETIC MUSICAL DANCING!

Nice consideration by you to check this guy!
    He is OK, Alright, Exercising but not too spry!
Had my salmon, peas and tomato-potato mix,
    That was good since my system is in this fix.

This morning I could read "The Economist!"
    Key articles on how will robots have ethics?
Now there are more problems for me to fix,
    Wondering is poetry on morality will work?

Had two hours preparing lesson for tonight,
    More questions than answers just what I like!
Q is winning over A in my poetry on "Q&A!"
    Now I have more ammunition from Asia!

Taoists, Confucius, Buddhists and Hindus,
　　All had amazing insights for us to review.
I am recording their "Rules for Warriors"
　　Better than most management programs!

The wisdom of Eastern Sages amazes!
　　Hope my beard will absorb their insights.
Western arrogance may get us in trouble,
　　This Lone Ranger needs to ride into town!

Two dashes of Buddha, meat from Jesus,
　　Plus Hindu peppers to be a vegetarian!
Then Shinto dessert, Tea of South India,
　　Side dish from Spinning Sufis for show!

Now update from workers inside house,
　　They are fixing what now is needed quietly.
Back tomorrow with owner coming again,
　　They are the team to get things all done!

Now for specials for you as of now today:
　　Boxes were picked up and receipt is OK!
Even angels can rest when they sweat,
　　So moderate your furious "get on with it!"

Rome was not built in a day, nor Ioway,
　　Pray for Wisconsin voters voting today!
TV, radio and press work up audiences,
　　But do not believe everything they give!

I have even more verses to compose,
　　Last night I thought of adding scores---
Those are musical scores combined,
　　Enriching each other by poetic wisdom!

You could think of dancing with stars,
　　Who read poetry with their own voices!
Rodgers and Hammerstein know how,
　　So Carol and Jerry create a new show!

As you know, it is healthy to dream!
　　Enriches our sleep with entertainment!
We could go on our world-wide tour,
　　Inviting universal peace and goodwill!

Does this make you sense opportunities?
　　We could travel to all the world's cities!
New CD's and IPODs to also broadcast,
　　All we need to do what we just imagine!

WHAT ARE YOU DOING THE REST OF YOUR LIFE?

Barbra Streisand

What are you doing the rest of your life
North and South and
East and West of your life
I have only one request of your life
That you spend it all with me
All the seasons and the times of your days
Are the nickels and the dimes of your days
Let the reasons and the rhymes of your days
All begin and end with me

I want to see your face in every kind of light
In fields of gold and forests of the night
And when you stand
Before the candles on a cake
Oh, let me be the one to hear
The silent wish you make.

Those tomorrows waiting deep in your…

Those tomorrows waiting deep in your eyes
In a world of love you keep in your eyes
I'll awaken what's asleep in your eyes
It may take a kiss or two

Through all of my life
Summer, winter, spring and fall of my life
All I ever will recall of my life
Is all my life with you

Source: LyricFind

IV. FAVORITES

O LOVE THAT WILT LET ME GO! [21]

O love, that wilt let me go:

    I rest my weary soul in Thee!

      I give Thee back the life I owe,

        That in thine ocean depth its flow,

          May richer an also fuller be.

          O light that followest all my way,

      I yield my flickering torch to Thee.

    My hears restores its borrowed ray,

  That in thy sunshine's blaze its day

My brighter, fairer be!

O Joy, that seekest me through pain,

    I cannot close my hear to Thee;

      I trace the rainbow though the rain,

        And feel the promise is not vain

          That morn shall fearless be!

          Oh, cross that liftest up my head;

      I dare not ask to fly from Thee.

---

[21] George Matheson (1882) and Albert Lister Peace (1884).,

I lay in dust life's glory dead,

And from the ground there blossoms red,

Life that shall endless be!

O Holy Night by **Mariah Carey**
O holy night, the stars are brightly shining
It is the night of our dear Savior's birth
Long lay the world, in sin and error pining
'Til He appeared and the soul felt its worth

A thrill of hope, the weary world rejoices
For yonder breaks, a new and glorious morn

Fall on your knees
O hear the angels' voices
O night divine
O night when Christ was born
O night divine
O night
O night divine

A thrill of hope, the weary world rejoices
For yonder breaks, a new and glorious morn

Fall on your knees
O hear the angels' voices
O night divine
O night when Christ was born
O night divine
O night...

Fall on your knees
O hear the angels' voices
O night divine
O night when Christ was born

O night divine
O night divine (O night divine)

Ooh, yes it was (O night divine)
Yeah, that is that night of our dear Savior's birth
(O night divine) oh yeah, oh yeah, oh yeah, yeah, yeah
(O night divine) it was a holy, holy, holy, oh, oh, oh
(O night divine) yes, it was

Source: <u>LyricFind</u>"

MORE[22]

More than the greatest love the world has known,

This is the love I'll give to you alone!

I only live to love you more each day,

More than you'll ever know!

My life will be in your keeping, waking, sleeping, laughing, weeping!

But far beyond forever you'll ever know,

More than You'll ever know, my arms long to hold you so.

My life will be in your keeping, waking, sleeping, weeping

GOD'S GREAT COMMANDMENT

What does God expect now from us, His People?

What does God expect of His Own Creation?

---

[22] Theme from "Mondo Cane"

To love mercy, to do justice, to walk humbly;[23]

Loving with all our heart is God's Command!

You endowed us, O God, with brain and mind,

Amazingly, you made us in Your Very Likeness.

What now do you require of us, Your People, O God?

To love you with all our mind is Your Command.

Your created us with Your MIghty Power and Will,

How then should we employ such awesome gifts?

Should we use such power for our own self-interests?

We should love each other with strength and soul!

You love us unconditionally, so should we express our love,

With all our heart, our mind, our strength, our very soul.

Loving You and our neighbor just as we love ourselves,

Loving our neighbor, ourselves and you our Faithful God.

To seek peace and just so now to live together,

Investing our energy, our efforts, our love and our time.

Sharing hope, freedom and justice sustains Your Peace,

By loving neighbor, self, and You as Our Eternal God.

---

[23] Micah 6: 6-8.

GOD'S EMOTIONS

Christians hold that God is all-knowing,

Does God know when we are emoting?

He is Loving, but does He know fearing?

How does <u>THE BIBLE</u> handle revealing?

In the <u>Old Testament</u> are "The Psalms,"[24]

Many chapters help us to stay calm.

An excellent balance for our gloom,

To experience balance for our scorn.

Yes, Scriptures do reveal God's anger! [25]

We may hope that He would be kinder!

Yes, God's outrage gets our attention;

What irritates God wo show revulsion?

We all benefit from "Emotional Intelligence."[26]

Even when we emote with our reluctance.

But emotions are not a disturbance,

Rather helping us express kindness!

---

[24] Psalm 23 and 6: 1.

[25] Exodus 5: 12, 4: 14, 32: 22; Numbers 32 1-14.

[26] Coleman, D., 1995, <u>Emotional Intelligence,</u> Batam Books, New York.

PSALM 90

God is my refuge and my dwelling place!

I can seek comfort and joy with my Lord!

Within His safety, this is my own residence,

Fearful anxieties are overcome with my God!

I will return to dust found on earth!

My time has limits, but God is Eternal!

This Psalm provides me with security!

Assurance to be with Him in Eternity!

On earth, let me make efforts to obey!

With awareness my life has few days!

PSALM 146

This is a Psalm praising God!

It is worthy of reading out-loud!

It recognizes Our Lord's Splendor!

Aware God is forever and forever!

This contrasts with human endeavors;

As we show our efforts to be electors.

Our governments have limitations;

As we try to exalt our own nations.

Our Righteous Lord is our model;

While recognizing we are fallible.

Love is exemplified by our Lord!

Not by rules of the human world.

God gives us the model of Jesus!

Hoping we show love that increases!

So may we try to reflect His Love!

Knowing Love comes from above!

A. ADDITIONAL LYRICS

"Who Can I Turn to When Nobody Needs Me?

My heart wants to know and so I must go

Where destiny leads me!" is a musical!

Single persons may decide to live alone;

Widows and widowers have lost someone;

Without their choice, they become lonesome!

Attraction has similarities to electrical magnetism;

While sexuality is a natural biological attraction.

Opposite sex utilizes biological identification!

Visual features accent what is noticed;

Vocalization seeks harmony accompanied!

Actions like dancing and kissing is affirmed!

Each species reproduces by sexual actions;

Some mate for a lifetime; others seek isolation.

Eventually, they need each other for reproduction!

TEAMWORK

Many species stay in joint unions;

Banning together for their protection;

In this teamwork, they have companions!

Ants are very notorious for their teamwork!

Protecting their colony is their major quirk!

Their Queen is the only one to shirk!

Human beings learn from ants and bees!

Honey bees signal directions as bee teams!

They jointly serve in their Queen's hives!

The skills of bees and ants are enviable!

Their "social intelligence" keeps them viable!

By working together by their being reliable!

BE OVER-JOYED!!!

Jesus brings us multiple gifts;

He arrives to be overjoyed!

He brings peace to be valued!

He brings hope to the discouraged!

Jesus demonstrated curiosities;

He opens to believers' possibilities.

So "rejoice" in the Lord always! [27]

Plus: "Again, I will say Rejoice!"

"Rejoice for what God has done,"

Plus, "Rejoice for what He will do!"

He heals all His Peoples' wounds.

With vaccines, He will come soon!

Mary's "My Soul magnified the Lord!"[28]

"And my Spirit rejoices in my God!"

"Release to the captives to be free!"

So recall God's promises of mercy!"

---

[27] Philippians 4: 4.
[28] Luke 1: 46-47, 15: 7.

PEACE OR PIECES?

Numerous wars are fought and lost!

Often resulting in winners and losers!

And rarely outcomes are "WIN-WIN!"

Neither do hostilities reach an end!

Revenge may seep during interludes

Hatred builds hostilities do not cease!

Illustrations exist among Europeans

France<>Germany<>Russia<>England

Angry tribes persist in the Middle East!

Families can be angry, hostile and mean!

More sedate are sporting rivalries!

Hoping rules will handle the "angries!"

Turning our focus on hot Middle East,

We can realize why war does not cease!

Thousands of years are often remembered!

Tensions build up so conflicts continue!

Generations learn about resentments!

Fueled to re-ignite in many moments!

Most American Presidents have attempted

To engage in some type of peace-making!

The Middle East has also created excuses

While negotiating for military resources!

Contributing more violence and abuses
While Middle East "Pieces need Peace!"

A. GLOBAL MUSIC

Cultures create their own melodies;
Global Music from many societies!
Citizens highly value their music;
They sing in private and in public!

Russians have distinctive music;
My visit highlighted this subject.
Russian Orthodox Churches example;
With their antiphonal choirs echoing.

In Russia, I also attended a classical opera;
Presented in Kremlin "The Barber of Seville!"
Previously, I had seen this opera in Vienna;
However, in Moscow it was mechanical!

Then St. Petersburg, it was a contrast;
"Mother Russia" carved in a huge statue.
Holding out her arms to her war dead;
Over half a million buried from WW II.

Russian classics are known worldwide;

"The 1812 Overture" is their pride.

This portrays the defense of Moscow

From Napoleon's attempt to invade.

African music is very distinctive;

I witnessed a burial procession.

Singers provided joyful melodies;

A burial was there a celebration!

Drums beaten loudly in Africa;

This set a pace for the procession.

People marching along to the beat;

This ceremony was very unique!

Japanese music is quite different;

Intoning rather somber sounds.

Only a few instruments involved;

Voices were much more subdued.

Chinese music is also distinctive;

I witnessed a fine Chinese Opera.

Players seemed to be mechanical;

The cast had to be very practical.

In Vietnam, we attended a concert;

The music was influenced by neighbors;

It also had clear American influence;

Due to the recent war settlements.

Music in India is very diverse;

Each region is quite dispersed;

Their chants provide verbal content;

Enriched with distinctive instruments.

Inner Venezuela had tribal ingredients;

The people from jungles were participants.

A limited range of instruments involved;

There a great many drums participated.

MUSIC BY LARGE ANIMALS

Most large animals respond to music!

The like rhythms with a big beat!

In Africa are giraffes and rhinos,

So big then might lift pianos!

The largest animals in Asia

Are elephants who carry loads.

Music helps them also to mellow

Moreover, Asia has water buffalo.

Antarctica has numerous penquins;

They are noted for how them swim!

South America has many tapirs;

North America has the bison!

Europe also has more bison;

North America has many buffalo!

These large animals love rhythms

To travel and also to then swim.

Big whales also construct songs! [29]

They communicate with music!

The Humpbacks listen to peers

The males master with ears!

Most human beings can hear whales;

David Rothenberg recorded renditions.

The lower tones travel further in water;

Songs typically are 5-30 minutes to hear!

Humpback whales do sing in higher tones

While Blue Whales sing in lower tones

!

---

[29] Welch, C. and Skerry, B., May, 2021, "The Secrets of the Whales," National Geographic, Ocean Issue.

Their songs might travel 125 miles!

We hear is influenced by waves!

Two Humpbacks sing together!

They may sing jointly for months.

Together they may change tunes,

As they sing in the sun and the moon.

CLASSICAL COMPOSITIONS

Beethoven's compositions are heavenly;

A bridge between baroque and classical.

Ludwig van Beethoven from Vienna;

Created piano scores for an organ.

Johann Sebastian Bach from Germany

Composed music for harp and organ.

His baroque music is well known;

Humanity is indebted to him.

Mozart's: <u>The Reign of Love!</u>

By age 6 he played the clavier!

Then stops and pedals Vienna;

By 1762, he played in Churches.

His Father saw him as miraculous!

In adulthood, classical music!

He composed for concerts and operas;

Then he became happily married!

MUSIC ABOUNDING!!

Music has multiple functions;

Bringing listeners into unions!

Vocal music is to harmonize;

Crescendos are no surprise!

Instruments blend into harmony;

Players join into a symphony!

Bands perform cooperatively;

Audiences respond delightfully!

Conductors heed musical scores;

They know when to signals raises.

Crescendos are for raising praises;

They sense when to do pauses!

Vocalists love to be singing;

Audiences also enjoy listening!

This interaction involves "coupling,"

Such duality prompts exchanging!

This blending becomes very fulfilling;

Performers are happy do blending;

All are encouraged to be engaged;

By being key members involved!

We call this "Music of the Spheres;"

Wherever sound waves are carried.

Singing and playing for vast hearers;

Blending chords that are musical!

Humans appreciate harmonious art;

Various participants become a part!

Performing requires key teamwork;

All joining into a musical concert!

All members of teams are valuable,

Individual contributions are critical.

"Music of the Spheres" is temporal;

Making "Heavenly Music" universal!

The great composers love Vienna;

"Vienna: the city of my Dreams!"

The Vienna Philharmonic Orchestra

Performs concerts outdoors in summer.

Listening to Vienna "Great Performances;"

Creates appreciation as music enhances!

My visits there include a classic opera

Plus, hearing Puccini and also "Zhivago!"

B. CORONAVIRUS IMPACT ON MUSIC

Music consoles many during coronavirus;

It has also impacted concerts for music!

Many Concert Halls have been closed!

Concert goers have fears they dread.

Since wearing masks are an imposition;

Covering nose and mouth for protection.

Musicians have become very frustrated;

Their own special art has been interrupted!

Recordings have been used to compensate

While live performances hope to wait!

Young performers are discouraged!

Their own talents are not appreciated!

COVID-19 threatens live performances; [30]

This stymies their future expectations.

What they enjoy is not cultivated;

Their careers have been stymied!

---

[30] Wilkins, G., February 14, 2021, <u>The Dallas Morning News.</u>

But musical appreciation continues;

Because its artistic beauty prevails!

Musicians are assets in society;

As compositions are lovely!

BLIND MUSICIANS

Blindness is compensated auditorially;

Lack of vision encourages dexterity.

This is displayed in a few pianists;

They may often perform as soloists!

As soloist relying upon coordination

Their keen brain guides their fingers.

They naturally impress hearers;

Who admire them as performers.

At a keyboard, they are amazing;

They may both be playing and singing!

Audiences respond by their clapping;

Players naturally find this encouraging.

Seeing displays comes from vision,

All six other senses typical in humans.

We are drawn to musical performances;

Humans fortunately have inheritances!

COMPOSERS

`Quinn Mason is a young composer;[31]

Creating symphonies for orchestras!

He heard all his music in his head

Then he learned how to record!

He studied at N. Dallas High School;

He has also learned to keep his cool!

With the Dallas Symphony Orchestra,

Plus, Seattle and Virginia Orchestras!

Prokofiev's "Peter and the Wolf,"

Fascinated his imagination.

He knows how to be creative;

Composing is very positive.

Quinn is a Black composer;

Nominated as Texan of 2020.

He is encouraged to compose;

At 24, unknown how far he goes!

---

[31] Editorial, December 31, 2020, The Dallas Morning News.

MUSICIANS NEED CREATIVE EQUITY

Musicians are often struggling artists;

They are treated unfairly by Economics![32]

Creative stars may not make a living;

Many musicians are not surviving!

This coronavirus has stymied their fans,

Concert Halls and Dance Halls closed down!

Audiences have been limited for protection;

Health concerns have placed limitations!

Song writers, musicians and composers

Have are some of the immediate losers!

Many have now been "kicked off the road!"

Staring into "the abyss of bank accounts!"

Artists demands are threaded with anxieties!

Understandably, they feel being treated unfairly!

Many musicians are unable to pursue a career;

Younger artists are face with major fears!

---

[32] Sisario, B., May 9, 2021, "Musicians Speak Up for Creative Equity, <u>The New York Times.</u>

MUSICAL MEDICINE
Healing Qualities of Music

Looking back over the years of 2020-21;
Benefits from displaying our empathy;
So many persons continue suffering
Their family and job face uncertainty.

Everyone faces a contagious illness;
This has been named coronavirus.
Schools and Businesses have adjusted,
Traveling plans have been rearranged.

Groups are meeting via ZOOM technology----
From Facebook and e-mail methodology;
Communicating and interacting regionally;
Permitting activities ahead internationally.

Humans have faced many sicknesses;
Leprosy, plagues, polio plus viruses;
We now have scientific medicines;
Prevention is helpful with vaccines.

Music provides many good effects;
Consequently, there are results!
Harmony beings us together;
The sick often feel better!

There are healing qualities from music;

Each song affects different body parts!

Esperanza Spalding's the "12 Little Spalts!" [33]

Bolstered results physically and emotionally!

She finds medicinal powers of music;

She "jammed" with a jazzy guitarist!

A beneficiary was like q wilted plant

Who found music was like watering.

Pandemic patients responded favorably;

In isolations, music helped positively.

Music therapists and neuroscientists

Refine the healing qualities of music.

Songwriters blend music with chants,

Music is beneficial for sick patients!

Listeners can select their favorites;

For both pleasure plus healing rites!

C. MUSIC: BEATING RHYTHMS!

The pace of music is noteworthy;

We humans feel this internally.

---

[33] Moore, M., April 2, 2021, "Her Quest Is for Musical Healing," <u>The New York Times.</u>

We sense our stride humanly

The "beat" felt unconsciously!

Note how listeners are responsive;

Body components become expressive.

Our head may show the rhythms;

From wagging heads to ear drums.

Conductors lead orchestras and bands;

Players guide their head and hands.

The audiences pick up the beat;

Watch how they move their feet.

Drummers carry out the rhythms;

Express beats for singers and players.

Cultures appreciate their drummers;

Drums constructed from their materials.

Responsive hearer show appreciation;

Reflected by their keen attention.

Participants value opportunities;

Uniquely expressed in communities.

INTIMATE TEAMING

Many species stay in natural unions;

Banning together for their protection!

In this teamwork, they have companions!

Ants are notorious for their teamwork!

Protecting their colony is their major quirk.

Their QUEEN is the only one who cannot shirk!

Human beings learn from ants and bees!

Honey bees signal directions to bee teams!

They jointly do serve their Queen's hives.

The skills of bees and ants are enviable!

Their "social intelligence keeps them viable!

By working together to become more reliable.

Nature teaches us to become adaptive;

Many species are ultimately creative!

Their impact upon us is positive!

ROMANTIC MUSCIAL LYRICS

"Who can I turn to when nobody needs me?"

My heart wants to know and so I must go

Where destiny leads me!" is a musical!

Single persons may decide to live alone;

Widows and widowers have lost someone.

Without their choice, they become lonesome.

Attraction has similarities to electrical magnetism;

While sexuality is a natural biological attraction.

Opposite sexes utilize biological identification!

Visual features assent what is noticed;

Vocalizations sees harmony accompanied!

Actions are dancing and kissing is affirmed!

Each species reproduces by sexual actions;

Some mate for a lifetime; others seek isolation.

Eventually they need each other for reproduction!

V. FAMOUS INSPIRATIONAL MUSIC:

The truth is that music is not just a melody;
    Music places life we cannot reach without it! [34]
        As music is a special place for us in time;
            Somewhere to go where no one else can.

            No noise, not interruptions can intrude;
        Closing us from the clamor of the Universe!
      Music gives us balm; it touches our souls.
Listeners discover warmth out of the cold!

Music is the prime sound to us from heaven!
      Saving us from the cacophony of the world!
        It crowds out noise to the orbit of the sublime!
            We can appreciate both music and our wine!

        We can play music often and repeatedly!
      Our memories, our hopes to be with God.
    Music gives us power to avoid distractions;
We often benefit from our new imaginations!

---

[34] Chittister, Joan, "The Places Life Cannot Reach Without It."

MAHATMA GANHDI UNIVERSITY

My host, Thomas John, made arrangements
That I speak at an Advent Worship Service.
The Chapel was filled to over-flowing
Persons listened in windows outside!

Attendance was in the range of 400-500;
This Christmas Service was a big occasion!
Carol came in December on her vacation!
We jointly enjoyed this special occasion!

Three years later, an invitation to Manipal U.
Arrangements to speak at eleven colleges!
The 9/11 attack came on New York City!
Carol bravely came on her vacation!

The Mar Thoma[35] Church Metropolitan
Invited me to speak at an Advent Service.
Their sanctuary was filled and people outside,
An estimate of 650-750 persons as worshipers!

A student ensemble of 10 sang vigorously,
This was also well attended by Rotarians;
They were many very actively participating;
Naturally the whole semester was exciting!

---

[35] Mar Thoma is translated a Saint Thomas.

TRAVELING IN INDIA

Can you recall roads you have traveled to bring back memories?
Good roads, bad roads, even dead-end roads that are shaky?
Older people recall mud-roads, gravel roads and bad rock roads!
Modern societies have tollroads and highways even abroad!

Probably the most frightening to us are very narrow roads,
Like mountain roads that have a precipice dropping to disasters!
I can recall Asian roads in China, India, Nepal, and Vietnam,
African roads in the Sahara Desert of Egypt and jungles of Ghana!

Poland highways took us to visit death camps of Auschwitz,
Plus, Russian roads to their ancient Capitol of Vladimiir-Suzdal.
But more memorable were the jungle roads below the Himalayas,
And taxi rides in the narrow India roads that were treacherous!

One of the curious signs on the bumpers of large wide trucks:
"HONK PLEASE!" so they would pull over to let fast cars pass!
But these very interesting experiences may just be distracting:
I want to focus on roads and paths are metaphors for describing!

Rotary International provided two grants,
To teach at a South India Universities!
In preparation, I enrolled in a Conference
Over 50,000 gathered in San Antonio!

Ned, a Friend, and I sang in a choir;

I sang bass and Ned sang tenor.

I met delegates from Manipal U.,

All of us all were surprised anew!

MUSIC IN THE MULTI-VERSES

Music of the expanding "multi-verse,"

Building on creation myths and sciences.

These multi-verse exists in space and time,

From what persists to what is sublime!

There may be a hundred billion galaxies; [36]

Stretching our human minds own qualities!

Quadrillion planets capable of supporting life!

From Aristarchus to the founding of Ptolemy!

Galileo turned the new telescope onto heavens;

He founded the new science particle mechanics!

These key discoveries helped Sir Isaac Newton

Who may be the greatest scientist known.

The observable universe over 100 billion,

Each with stars of another 100 billion.

46.5 billion light-years known in 2000;

Such distance is beyond our light horizon.

[36] Stenger, V., 2014, <u>God and the Multiverse,</u> Prometheus Books, New York.

The "Big Bang" really made a bang!

The cosmic microwaves exhibit tones!

Like musical instruments being played

With poor acoustics for good sound!

A. SYMPHONIC MUSIC

Directors of Symphony have a long tradition,

Many have been creators of compositions.

They comprehend their very own music;

Their "ownership" of their own classic!

These traditions have been ingrained;

Creators, performers and hearers claimed.

Symphonies are very complicated to perform

There are patterns to which they conform!

In recent decades, traditions are challenged;

Many orchestras have women who do play.

Yes, their talents now are not suppressed;

As both women and men do their best!

Diversity adds to recent performances;

Young players display their own talents!

Amazingly, they can master compositions!

No longer are these paternalistic traditions!

Now women are becoming Directors;[37]

Their talents build upon collectors.

The Baltimore Symphony is one;

Dallas Symphony at Meyerson!

BASS MUSIC HALL

Here we were in Bass Music Hall

Crowds come as musicians recall!

Scores and instrument performing!

We await the first move for listening.

Nice, tasteful decor outlines each wall!

Ceiling baffles blend into this hall!

Smaller percent of young present;

Persons over 50 are majority to listen!

Now the orchestra members quiet down!

The first violinist sets the pitch to blend!

The young conductor quietly appears;

"The Star Spangled Banner" sounds!

More women play with bow and violins!

Noticeable number of Asian-Americans!

---

[37] Woolfe, Z., June 6, 2021, "Passing the Baton to Conducting's Next Generation," The New York Times.

With dignity, 1st violinist sounds tonality

Leads all the sections into harmony!

Naturally, the horns sound prominently!

As all the trumpets sound very loudly!

Six bass strings for the lower ranges!

Then the percussion drummer booms!

My hearing aid has been turned off!

Their sounds may distort high tones!

Eight of ten first violinists are Japanese;

Four are women playing very at ease.

The pianist plays Bartok"s music capably!

Blending with the Orchestra beautifully.

The Director reveals his own great talent

This musical score certainly complements!

BRAHM'S SYMPHONY NO.1 IN C MINOR

This Ft. Worth Orchestra is memorable!

Conductor Christoph Konig is so vital!

He knows his composition thoroughly;

Directing all the sections from memory!

He does not even look at the score!

Allowing him to do even much more!

This Orchestra plays magnificently!

The audience responded appreciably!

Carol and I are both very enthralled!

In listening to Brahms in Bass Hall!

The concert was preceded by a lecture!

That provided all of us helpful pictures!

This experience was very fulfilling;

Such superb music is also thrilling.

Concerts are special experiences;

As musical qualities are significant!

MUSIC AT THE MEYERSON

Personal memories are from the MEYERSON;

This is a wonderful hall for classic music!

The Dallas Symphony fills my head!

With joyful music, my ears are filled!

One concert was Mozart's clarinet solo;

Plus, Schubert's "Unfinished Symphony!"

These compositions were enjoyable;

They help me find musicals fulfillable!

North Texas is fortunate to be blessed;

Top-notch music is heartily played!

The concerts are very contagious;

While hosting is very gracious!

Attending concerts is superb;

And dinners that are delicious!

These are wonderful combinations;

Contributing to musical appreciations.

THE HEALING POWER OF POETRY[38]

We know that our bodies at times need healing;

From injuries, ailments, fractures from falling.

Medicines may be the helpful treatment;

Illnesses show how fragile and faint!

We also may find poetic verses helpful!

Our ears may provide entry for recovery!

These words could be called "soul's talk!"

Along with exercise whenever we also walk!

Music and Poetry are both "healers!"

These compositions have "hearers!"

Many listeners find improvement

Their bodies love the movements!

---

[38] Judge, M., May 23, 2021, "The Healing Power of Poetry, <u>Dallas Morning News.</u>

These healing qualities show development;

Both physical and spiritual enhancement!

These may be recovering these qualities;

That have long been known in the Humanities!

B. LOVING-KINDNESS AS A PRESCRIPTION!

By doing deeds of kindness

Are a vitally good process!

Kindly deeds have influence

For good health as a difference!

Scientists are making discoveries

That helps us cope with loneliness!

Good deeds aid our immune system;

That can build up our resistance.

Lonely persons develop low myeloid cells;[39]

So, vulnerability develops to infection!

Since loneliness starts with solitude

Taking on a physiological life itself!

"Myeloid" feedback can do a loop;

Defensive suspicions can develop!

---

[39] Cole, Steven, April 18, 2020 "Immunity from being alone," <u>The Economist.</u>; Kuramoto, H., 2004, <u>International Journal of Biochemistry Cell.</u>

More than personal visits are needed

Ask lonely persons to do acts of kindness!

These kind actions may reduce Myeloids,

As well as to reduce their loneliness!

Plus, also making contributions;

Writing a note to a friend helps!

On-line kindness can be beneficial!

Making contact might be special!

Loving kindness is also <u>Biblical</u>[40]

A prescription worth a trial!

Blessed are voices for singing!

These enter our ears for ringing!

Taking us into musical spheres,

Melodies we hear in our ears.

Music does become inspirational![41]

These performances are emotional!

This poetry now focuses on music;

All types: pop, popular and classic!

---

[40] I Samuel 15: 6, Micah 6: 8, Romans 11: 22, Colossians 3: 12.

[41] Psalms 47, 59, 68, 96 104, 147, Isaiah 12: 5-6; I Corinthians 14: 15.

Spiritual hymns are widely sung;

With organs, pianos and drums!

Choirs, solos, whole congregations

They help us echo with inspiration!

Open our hearts, voices and ears;

Let us respond with joys and tears!

Even whales sing in the deep oceans;

Music touches our minds and emotions!

CARING RELATIONSHIPS[42]

Close relationships are invaluable;

For Loving Kindness we are able.

Marriage and romantic relations

Enhance partnership connections!

Shostrom developed an inventory;

Multiple Scales express this story!

He has contrasts of: "I-It" and "I-Thou" [43]

To reveal the qualities shown to you!

Shostrom also analyzed "Loving Kindness,"

With understandable scales useful to us.

---

[42]"Composing by Computer; Programmes by Programs," The Economist, June 5, 2021.
Shostrom, E, 1969, "Caring Relationship Inventory.
[43] Buber, M., "I-THOU"

"Eros" is a Greek term for showing love;

"Amour" is a flirtatious expression!

"Agape" is self-giving love!

Demonstrated in Jesus' love!

Self-Love is also very important

To help see them as significant!

As humans, we are capable of all;

We can express these at will.

Since mutual love is hopeful

Experienced as wonderful!

Life is becoming enhanced!

Complex life is being advanced!

Physically, mentally and spiritually

All life benefits with talents musically!

OUR SONNET TO MISS KAITLIN![44]

News from you has been Wonderful!

Your enthusiasm is apparent so we are also Joyful!

What a splendor for you Carol and I to start on this Friday!

---

[44] Our youngest granddaughter.

Isn't it exhilarating to be excited?

    Your patient determination has surely been tested!

        Two options in hand that means batting 110%!

OK, our math is slightly overstated!

    Our poetic verses permit this type of verbal license!

        We rejoice in your acceptances for you to now choose!

For two years reveal you as intense!

    Your focused attention to work, study and contests!

        We celebrate your successful accomplishment!

Carol and I remember your birth,

    Your arrival had all awaiting your inauguration!

        Your head of hair and dark eyes were an exploration!

We imagine your parents are proud,

    Daughter, 28, is planning this big transition,

        The energy you invest reveals your determination!

No doubt you have many dreams,

    That process your aspirations in deep streams!

        It is apparent imagination give you motivation!

We're pleased you have two options!

    Better decisions are possible with due evaluation!

        McMurray U. and Southwestern U. is a privilege!

These universities are well known,

    Both have roots in Christian focus on education!

        A century ago, key schools were on the frontier!

Having your own preferences is a key,

    As a young adult you are blessed with privileges!

        Your parents have sacrificed to provide these opportunities.

Carol and I once were both very young!

    At 16 years we also were given new undertakings!

        You had teachers and parents working together!

Socrates, the Greek gave his advice:

    "Always remember your teachers!" all your life!

        These are many adults plus your sister to name just a few.

Education is recognized as essential,

    To help students like you reach your potential!

        I have messages from former students with gratitude!

Creative students like you are a blessing,

You "turn on" teachers plus also your classmates!

A few insights from 63 years as a Minister<>Professor:

Creative persons thrive in environments,

That challenge you with opportunities to pursue!

You decide about college where you flourish!

Know yourself in these new environments!

Those that "turn you on" have the greatest promise!

Wonder if you will be proud as a graduate!

We trust that God continues to bless you!

As our gift from The Divine, we rejoice with you!

Keep us aware of your joys and eventual challenges!

"WITH A SONG IN MY HEART"[45]

Music for a person has a beginning;

Females often start by humming!

While male may start by whistling!

In times, both begin also singing!

In private, both may do exploring,

Their personal preferences expanding!

Duets, trios, quartettes and choirs

Voices develop as a person aspires!

Musical instruments are appealing

Individual, bands or orchestrating!

Persons want the best for developing

A they decide what is improving!

Music has appeals for development;

Regular practice leads to enhancement.

Hopefully pursued for real enjoyment;

The best may lead to employment!

Human musical gifts are inspirational;

Thrilling are mind and body auditorial.

---

[45] Rodgers, R. and Hart, 1929,

Composers' talents are appreciated;
Performers make hearers existed!

Executing scores is a real challenge;
    This is greater than hearers imagine.
        Players engage in years of practice,
            Discipline needed to do exercises!

            Composers and performers are valued!
        With our ears and hearts appreciated
    As they share what has been composed.
All humanity is thereby also blessed!

Handel's "Messiah," is an outstanding chorus;
    Powerfully includes "Hosana" in the highest! [46]
        Hallelujah, AMEN; Hallelujah, AMEN; Hallelujah!
            Let us rejoice in singing this inspiring chorus!

---

[46] Handel, G, F. 1742

BIBLIOGRAPHY

Armstrong, Karen

Augustine, <u>Confessions of St. Augustine.</u> Plus Ruth 2: 14-23 and Titus 3: 4-6.

Bach, Johann Sebastian was the famous composer.

Cole, Steven, April 18, 2020 "Immunity from being alone," <u>The Economist.;</u> Kuramoto, H., 2004, <u>International Journal of Biochemistry Cell.</u>

"Composing by Computer; Programmes by Programs," <u>The Economist</u>, June 5, 2021.

Editorial, December 31, 2020, <u>The Dallas Morning News.</u>

Handel, G., F., 1742, "The Messiah," <u>New Testament.</u>

Hernanadez, J., July 2, 2021, :State-Approved Music Fills Lineup of Events," <u>New York Times.</u>

Houston-Edwards, K., April 2021, <u>Scientific American.</u>

Judge, M., May 23, 2021, "The Healing Power of Poetry, <u>Dallas Morning News.</u>

Kale, Claudia, May 2021, "Bridging Cultures and Good Causes with Music," <u>National Geographic.</u>

Levitin, D., 8/25, 2016, "Where Word Fail, Music Speaks,"

Matheson, G., (1882) and Albert Lister Peace (1884).

Middents, G., 2004, Sung at the Global Meeting of the Organizational Development Institute, U. of Colima, Mexico.

Ibid. 2020, SPORTS amd RELIGIONS, iUniverse Books.

Moore, M., April 2, 2021, "Her Quest Is for Musical Healing," The New York Times.

Nichols, M. and Straus, M., 2021, The Lost Art of Listening Guilford Press.

Pinker, S., 2013, Language, Cognition and Human Nature, Oxford University Press.

Psalms 47, 59, 68, 96 104, 147, Isaiah 12: 5-6; I Corinthians 14: 15.

The Presbyterian Hymnal, 1990, "Christmas Music, Westminster John Knox Press.

Rodgers, R., and Hart, 1929,

Shostrom, E., 1969, "Caring Relationship Inventory."

Sisario, B., May 9, 2021, "Musicians Speak Up for Creative Equity, The New York Times.

Stenger, V., 2014, God and the Multiverse, Prometheus Books, New York.

Swafford, J., "Mozart: The Reign of Love," Faber and Faber.

Welch, C. and Skerry, B., May, 2021, "The Secrets of the Whales," National Geographic, Ocean Issue.

Wilkins, G., February 14, 2021, The Dallas Morning News.

Woolfe, Z., June 6, 2021, "Passing the Baton to Conducting's Next Generation," New York Times.

Printed in the United States
by Baker & Taylor Publisher Services

Printed in the United States
by Baker & Taylor Publisher Services